3/99

Revolutionary Petunias
& Other Poems

BOOKS BY ALICE WALKER

*Once: Poems*

*The Third Life of Grange Copeland*

*Revolutionary Petunias & Other Poems*

*In Love & Trouble: Stories of Black Women*

*Langston Hughes, American Poet*

*Meridian*

*I Love Myself When I Am Laughing . . .*
*A Zora Neale Hurston Reader* (editor)

*Good Night, Willie Lee, I'll See You in the Morning*

*You Can't Keep a Good Woman Down: Stories*

*The Color Purple*

*In Search of Our Mothers' Gardens: Womanist Prose*

*Horses Make a Landscape Look More Beautiful*

*To Hell with Dying* (illustrations by Catherine Deeter)

*Living by the Word*

*The Temple of My Familiar*

*Her Blue Body Everything We Know:*
*Earthling Poems 1965–1990 Complete*

*Finding the Green Stone*
(illustrations by Catherine Deeter)

*Possessing the Secret of Joy*

# Revolutionary Petunias
# & Other Poems
## *by Alice Walker*

A Harvest Book
Harcourt Brace & Company
*San Diego   New York   London*

Requests for permission to make copies of any part of the work
should be mailed to:
Permissions Department, Harcourt Brace & Company,
8th Floor, Orlando, Florida 32887.

Some of these poems previously appeared in *Freedomways*,
*Harper's*, *Essence*, and *Black World*.

Library of Congress Catalog Card Number 72-88796
ISBN 0-15-676620-5 (pbk.)

Printed in the United States of America

K L M N O

*Humbly for George Jackson, who could "still smile
sometimes. . . ." Whose eyes warmed to life until
the end; whose face was determined, unconquered,
and sweet.*

*And for my heroes, heroines, and friends of
early SNCC whose courage and beauty burned me
forever.*

*And for the Mississippi Delta legend of
Bob Moses.*

*And for Winson Hudson and Fannie Lou Hamer
whose strength and compassion I cherish.*

*And for my friend, Charles Merrill, the artist, who
paints skies.*

*And for Mel, the Trouper's father, who daily
fights and daily loves, from a great heart.*

These poems are about Revolutionaries and
Lovers; and about the loss of compassion, trust,
and the ability to expand in love that marks the
end of hopeful strategy. Whether in love or
revolution. They are also about (and for) those
few embattled souls who remain painfully committed
to beauty and to love even while facing the
firing squad.

—Alice Walker

# Contents

Revolutionary Petunias
& Other Poems

# In These Dissenting Times

> *To acknowledge our ancestors means*
> *we are aware that we did not make*
> *ourselves, that the line stretches*
> *all the way back, perhaps, to God; or*
> *to Gods. We remember them because it*
> *is an easy thing to forget: that we*
> *are not the first to suffer, rebel,*
> *fight, love and die. The grace with*
> *which we embrace life, in spite of*
> *the pain, the sorrows, is always a*
> *measure of what has gone before.*
>
> —Alice Walker, "Fundamental Difference"

# IN THESE DISSENTING TIMES

I shall write of the old men I knew
And the young men
I loved
And of the gold toothed women
Mighty of arm
Who dragged us all
To church.

## THE OLD MEN USED TO SING

The old men used to sing
And lifted a brother
Carefully
Out the door
I used to think they
Were born
Knowing how to
Gently swing
A casket
They shuffled softly
Eyes dry
        More awkward
With the flowers
Than with the widow
After they'd put the
Body in
And stood around waiting
In their
Brown suits.

WINKING AT A FUNERAL

Those were the days
Of winking at a
Funeral
Romance blossomed
In the pews
Love signaled
Through the
Hymns
What did we know?

Who smelled the flowers
Slowly fading
Knew the arsonist
Of the church?

III

WOMEN

They were women then
My mama's generation
Husky of voice— Stout of
Step
With fists as well as
Hands
How they battered down
Doors
And ironed
Starched white
Shirts
How they led
Armies
Headragged Generals
Across mined
Fields
Booby-trapped
Ditches
To discover books
Desks
A place for us
How they knew what we
*Must* know
Without knowing a page
Of it
Themselves.

## THREE DOLLARS CASH

Three dollars cash
For a pair of catalog shoes
Was what the midwife charged
My mama
For bringing me.
"We wasn't so country then," says Mom,
"You being the last one—
And we couldn't, like
We done
When she brought your
Brother,
Send her out to the
Pen
And let her pick
Out
A pig."

V

YOU HAD TO GO
TO FUNERALS

You had to go to funerals
Even if you didn't know the
People
Your Mama always did
Usually your Pa.
In new patent leather shoes
It wasn't so bad
And if it rained
The graves dropped open
And if the sun was shining
You could take some of the
Flowers home
In your pocket
book. At six and seven
The face in the gray box
Is always your daddy's
Old schoolmate
Mowed down before his
Time.
You don't even ask
After a while
What makes them lie so
Awfully straight
And still. If there's a picture of
Jesus underneath

The coffin lid
You might, during a boring sermon,
Without shouting or anything,
Wonder who painted it;

And how *he* would like
All eternity to stare
It down.

VI

UNCLES

They had broken teeth
And billy club scars
But we didn't notice
Or mind
They were uncles.
It was their *job*
To come home every summer
From the North
And tell my father
He wasn't no man
And make my mother
Cry and long
For Denver, Jersey City,
Philadelphia.
They were uncles.
Who noticed how
Much
They drank
And acted womanish
With they do-rags
We were nieces.
And they were almost
Always good
For a nickel
Sometimes
a dime.

THEY TAKE A LITTLE NIP

They take a little nip
Now and then
Do the old folks

Now they've moved to
Town
You'll sometimes
See them sitting
Side by side
On the porch

Straightly
As in church

Or working diligently
Their small
City stand of
Greens

Serenely pulling
Stalks and branches
Up
Leaving all
The weeds.

VIII

SUNDAY SCHOOL, CIRCA 1950

"Who made you?" was always
The question
The answer was always
"God."
Well, there we stood
Three feet high
Heads bowed
Leaning into
Bosoms.

Now
I no longer recall
The Catechism
Or brood on the Genesis
Of life
No.

I ponder the exchange
Itself
And salvage mostly
The leaning.

# Burial

They have fenced in the dirt road
that once led to Wards Chapel
A.M.E. church,
and cows graze
among the stones that
mark my family's graves.
The massive oak is gone
from out the church yard,
but the giant space is left
unfilled;
despite the two-lane blacktop
that slides across
the old, unalterable
roots.

II

Today I bring my own child here;
to this place where my father's
grandmother rests undisturbed
beneath the Georgia sun,
above her the neatstepping hooves
of cattle.
Here the graves soon grow back into the land.
Have been known to sink. To drop open without

warning. To cover themselves with wild ivy,
blackberries. Bittersweet and sage.
No one knows why. No one asks.
When Burning Off Day comes, as it does
some years,
the graves are haphazardly cleared and snakes
hacked to death and burned sizzling
in the brush. . . . The odor of smoke, oak
leaves, honeysuckle.
Forgetful of geographic resolutions as birds,
the farflung young fly South to bury
the old dead.


III

The old women move quietly up
and touch Sis Rachel's face.
"Tell Jesus I'm coming," they say.
"Tell Him I ain't goin' to *be*
long."

My grandfather turns his creaking head
away from the lavender box.
He does not cry. But looks afraid.
For years he called her "Woman";
shortened over the decades to
" 'Oman."
On the cut stone for " 'Oman's" grave
he did not notice
they had misspelled her name.


13

(The stone reads *Racher Walker*—not "Rachel"—
*Loving Wife, Devoted Mother.*)


IV


As a young woman, who had known her? Tripping
eagerly, "loving wife," to my grandfather's
bed. Not pretty, but serviceable. A hard
worker, with rough, moist hands. Her own two
babies dead before she came.
*Came to seven children.*
*To aprons and sweat.*
*Came to quiltmaking.*
*Came to canning and vegetable gardens*
*big as fields.*
*Came to fields to plow.*
*Cotton to chop.*
*Potatoes to dig.*
*Came to multiple measles, chickenpox,*
*and croup.*
*Came to water from springs.*
*Came to leaning houses one story high.*
*Came to rivalries. Saturday night battles.*
*Came to straightened hair, Noxzema, and*
*feet washing at the Hardshell Baptist church.*
*Came to zinnias around the woodpile.*
*Came to grandchildren not of her blood*
*whom she taught to dip snuff without*
*sneezing.*

*Came to death blank, forgetful of it all.*

*When he called her " 'Oman" she no longer*
*listened. Or heard, or knew, or felt.*


V


It is not until I see my first grade teacher
review her body that I cry.
Not for the dead, but for the gray in my
first grade teacher's hair. For memories
of before I was born, when teacher and
grandmother loved each other; and later
above the ducks made of soap and the orange-
legged chicks Miss Reynolds drew over
my own small hand
on paper with wide blue lines.


VI


Not for the dead, but for memories. None of
them sad. But seen from the angle of her
death.


15

## For My Sister Molly Who in the Fifties

Once made a fairy rooster from
Mashed potatoes
Whose eyes I forget
But green onions were his tail
And his two legs were carrot sticks
A tomato slice his crown.
Who came home on vacation
When the sun was hot
and cooked
and cleaned
And minded least of all
The children's questions
A million or more
Pouring in on her
Who had been to school
And knew (and told us too) that certain
Words were no longer good
And taught me not to say us for we
No matter what "Sonny said" up the
road.


FOR MY SISTER MOLLY WHO IN THE FIFTIES
Knew Hamlet well and read into the night
And coached me in my songs of Africa
A continent I never knew
But learned to love
Because "they" she said could carry

16

A tune
And spoke in accents never heard
In Eatonton.
Who read from *Prose and Poetry*
And loved to read "Sam McGee from Tennessee"
On nights the fire was burning low
And Christmas wrapped in angel hair
And I for one prayed for snow.


WHO IN THE FIFTIES
Knew all the written things that made
Us laugh and stories by
The hour        Waking up the story buds
Like fruit. Who walked among the flowers
And brought them inside the house
And smelled as good as they
And looked as bright.
Who made dresses, braided
Hair. Moved chairs about
Hung things from walls
Ordered baths
Frowned on wasp bites
And seemed to know the endings
Of all the tales
I had forgot.

        *

WHO OFF INTO THE UNIVERSITY
Went exploring        To London and
To Rotterdam

Prague and to Liberia
Bringing back the news to us
Who knew none of it
But followed
crops and weather
funerals and
Methodist Homecoming;
easter speeches,
*groaning* church.


WHO FOUND ANOTHER WORLD
Another life        With gentlefolk
Far less trusting
And moved and moved and changed
Her name
And sounded precise
When she spoke        And frowned away
Our sloppishness.


WHO SAW US SILENT
Cursed with fear        A love burning
Inexpressible
And sent me money not for me
But for "College."
Who saw me grow through letters
The words misspelled        But not
The longing        Stretching
Growth
The tied and twisting

Tongue
Feet no longer bare
Skin no longer burnt against
The cotton.


WHO BECAME SOMEONE OVERHEAD
A light        A thousand watts
Bright and also blinding
And saw my brothers cloddish
And me destined to be
Wayward
My mother remote        My father
A wearisome farmer
With heartbreaking
Nails.


FOR MY SISTER MOLLY WHO IN THE FIFTIES
Found much
Unbearable
Who walked where few had
Understood        And sensed our
Groping after light
And saw some extinguished
And no doubt mourned.

FOR MY SISTER MOLLY WHO IN THE FIFTIES
Left us.

         * *


19

## Eagle Rock

In the town where I was born
There is a mound
Some eight feet high
That from the ground
Seems piled up stones
In Georgia
Insignificant.

But from above
The lookout tower
Floor
An eagle widespread
In solid gravel
Stone
Takes shape
Below;

The Cherokees raised it
Long ago
Before westward journeys
In the snow
Before the
National Policy slew
Long before Columbus knew.

I used to stop and
Linger there
Within the cleanswept tower stair

Rock Eagle pinesounds
Rush of stillness
Lifting up my hair.

Pinned to the earth
The eagle endures
The Cherokees are gone
The people come on tours.
And on surrounding National
Forest lakes the air rings
With cries
The silenced make.

Wearing cameras
They never hear
But relive their victory
Every year
And take it home
With them.
Young Future Farmers
As paleface warriors
Grub
Live off the land
Pretend Indian, therefore
Man,
Can envision a lake
But never a flood
On earth
So cleanly scrubbed
Of blood:

They come before the rock
Jolly conquerers.

They do not know the rock
They love
*Lives* and is bound
To bide its time
To wrap its stony wings
Around
The innocent eager 4-H Club.

# Baptism

*They dunked me in the creek;*
*a tiny brooklet.*
*Muddy, gooey with rotting leaves,*
*a greenish mold floating;*
*definable.*
*For love it was. For love of God*
*at seven. All in white.*
*With God's mud ruining my snowy*
*socks and his bullfrog spoors*
*gluing up my face.*

## J, My Good Friend (another foolish innocent)

It is too easy not to like
Jesus,
It worries greatness
To an early grave
Without any inkling
Of what is wise.

So when I am old,
And so foolish with pain
No one who knows
me
Can tell from which
Senility or fancy
I deign to speak,
I may sing
In my cracked and ugly voice
Of Jesus my good
Friend;
Just as the old women
In my home town
Do now.

# View from Rosehill Cemetery: Vicksburg

*for Aaron Henry*

Here we have watched ten thousand
seasons
come and go.
And unmarked graves atangled
in the brush
turn our own legs to trees
vertical forever between earth
and sun.
Here we are not quick to disavow
the pull of field and wood
and stream;
we are not quick to turn
upon our dreams.

# Revolutionary Petunias

*for June and Julius*

*Beauty, no doubt, does not make
revolutions. But a day will come when
revolutions will have need of beauty.*

—Albert Camus, *The Rebel*

Sammy Lou of Rue
sent to his reward
the exact creature who
murdered her husband,
using a cultivator's hoe
with verve and skill;
and laughed fit to kill
in disbelief
at the angry, militant
pictures of herself
the Sonneteers quickly drew:
not any of them people that
she knew.
A backwoods woman
her house was papered with
funeral home calendars and
faces appropriate for a Mississippi
Sunday School. She raised a George,
a Martha, a Jackie and a Kennedy. Also
a John Wesley Junior.
"Always respect the word of God,"
she said on her way to she didn't
know where, except it would be by
electric chair, and she continued
"Don't yall forgit to *water*
my purple petunias."

## Expect Nothing

Expect nothing. Live frugally
On surprise.
Become a stranger
To need of pity
Or, if compassion be freely
Given out
Take only enough
Stop short of urge to plead
Then purge away the need.

Wish for nothing larger
Than your own small heart
Or greater than a star;
Tame wild disappointment
With caress unmoved and cold
Make of it a parka
For your soul.

Discover the reason why
So tiny human midget
Exists at all
So scared unwise
But expect nothing. Live frugally
On surprise.

# Be Nobody's Darling

*for Julius Lester*


Be nobody's darling;
Be an outcast.
Take the contradictions
Of your life
And wrap around
You like a shawl,
To parry stones
To keep you warm.

Watch the people succumb
To madness
With ample cheer;
Let them look askance at you
And you askance reply.

Be an outcast;
Be pleased to walk alone
(Uncool)
Or line the crowded
River beds
With other impetuous
Fools.

Make a merry gathering
On the bank
Where thousands perished

For brave hurt words
They said.

Be nobody's darling;
Be an outcast.
Qualified to live
Among your dead.

# Reassurance

I must love the questions
themselves
as Rilke said
like locked rooms
full of treasure
to which my blind
and groping key
does not yet fit.

and await the answers
as unsealed
letters
mailed with dubious intent
and written in a very foreign
tongue.

and in the hourly making
of myself
no thought of Time
to force, to squeeze
the space
I grow into.

## Nothing Is Right

Nothing is right
that does not work.
We have believed it all:
improvement, progress,
bigger, better, immediate,
fast.
The whole Junk.

It was our essence that
never worked.
We hasten to eradicate
our selves.

Consider the years
of rage and wrench and
mug.
What was it kept
the eyes alive?
Declined to outmode
the
hug?

# Crucifixions

*I am not an idealist, nor a cynic,*
*but merely unafraid of contradictions.*
*I have seen men face each other when*
*both were right, yet each was determined*
*to kill the other, which was wrong.*
*What each man saw was an image of the*
*other, made by someone else. That is*
*what we are prisoners of.*

—A personal testament by Donald Hogan,
   *Harper's Magazine*, January, 1972

# Black Mail

Stick the finger inside
the chink;
nail long and sharp.
Wriggle it,
*jugg*,
until it draws blood.
Lick it in your mouth,
savor the taste;
and know your diet
has changed.

Be the first at the crucifixion.
Stand me (and them and her and him)
where once we each together
stood.
Find it plausible now
to jeer,
escaped within your armor.
There never was a crucifixion
of a completely armored man.

Imagine this: a suit of mail,
of metal plate;
no place to press the dagger in.
Nothing but the eyes
to stick
with narrow truth.

Burning sharp,
burning bright;
burning righteous,
but burning blind.

# Lonely Particular

When the people knew you
That other time
You were not as now
A crowding General,
Firing into your own
Ranks;
Forcing the tender skin
Of men
Against the guns
The very sun
To mangled perfection
For your cause.

Not General then
But frightened boy.
The cheering fell
Within the quiet
That fed your
Walks
Across the mines.
A mere foot soldier,
Marching the other way;
A lonely Particular.

# Perfection

Having reached perfection
as you have
there no longer exists
the need for love.
Love is ablution
the dirtied is due
the sinner can
use.

# The Girl Who Died #1

"Look!" she cried.
"I am not perfect
but still your sister.
*Love me!*"
But the mob beat her and kicked her
and shaved her head;
until she saw exactly
how wrong she was.

# Ending

I so admired you then;
before the bloody ending
of the story
cured your life
of all belief.
I would have wished
you alive
still. Or even
killed.
Before this thing we
got,
with flailing arms
and venomous face
took our love away.

# Lost My Voice? Of Course.   /  for Beanie*

Lost my voice?
Of course.

You said "Poems of
love and flowers are
a luxury the Revolution
cannot afford."

Here are the warm and juicy
vocal cords,
slithery,
from my throat.

Allow me to press them upon
your fingers,
as you have pressed
that bloody voice of yours
in places it could not know
to speak,
nor how to trust.

* A childhood bully.

## The Girl Who Died #2    / for d.p.

No doubt she was a singer
of naughty verse
and hated judgments
(black and otherwise)
and wove a life
of stunning contradiction,
was driven mad
by obvious
professions
and the word
"sister"
hissed by snakes
belly-low,
poisonous,
in the grass.
Waiting with sex
or tongue
to strike.

Behold the brothers!

They strut behind
the casket
wan and sad
and murderous.
Thinking whom
to blame
for making this girl

die
alone, lashed
denied
into her room.

This girl who would not lie;
and was not born
to be "correct."

## The Old Warrior Terror

Did you hear?
After everything
the Old Warrior Terror
died a natural death at home,
in bed.
Just reward
for having proclaimed abroad
that True Believers never
doubt;
True Revolutionaries never
smile.

## Judge Every One with Perfect Calm

Follow the train full of bodies;
listening in the tiny wails
for reassurance of your mighty
right. Ride up and down the gorges
on your horse
collecting scalps.
Your creed is simple, and even
true: We learn from each other
by doing. Period.

Judge every one with perfect calm.
Stand this man here and that one
there;
mouths begging open holes.
Let them curtsey into the ditch
dug before them.
They will not recall tomorow
your judgment of today.

# The QPP

The quietly pacifist peaceful
always die
to make room for men
who shout. Who tell lies to
children, and crush the corners
off of old men's dreams.
And now I find your name,
scrawled large in someone's
blood, on this survival
list.

# He Said Come

He said come
Let me exploit you;
Somebody must do it
And wouldn't you
Prefer a brother?
Come, show me your
Face,
All scarred with tears;
Unburden your heart—
Before the opportunity
Passes away.

*. . . Or maybe the purpose of being
here, wherever we are, is to increase
the durability and the occasions of
love among and between peoples. Love,
as the concentration of tender caring
and tender excitement, or love as the
reasons for joy. I believe that love
is the single, true prosperity of any
moment and that whatever and whoever
impedes, diminishes, ridicules, opposes
the development of loving spirit is
"wrong"/hateful.*

— June Jordan

## Mysteries

*The man who slowly walked away from
them was a king in their society. A day
had come when he had decided that he
did not need any kingship other than the
kind of wife everybody would loathe
from the bottom of their hearts. He had
planned for that loathing in secret;
they had absorbed the shock in secret.
When everything was exposed, they had
only one alternative: to keep their preju-
dice and pretend Maru had died.*

— Bessie Head, *Maru*

51

MYSTERIES


Your eyes are widely open flowers.
Only their centers are darkly clenched
To conceal Mysteries
That lure me to a keener blooming
Than I know,
And promise a secret
I must have.

I

the gift he gave unknowing
she already had
though feebly
lost
a planted thing
within herself
scarcely green
nearly severed

till he came

a magic root
sleeping beneath
branches
long grown wild.

II

and when she thought of him
seated in the dentist's chair
she thought she understood
the hole she
discovered through
her tongue
as mysteries in
separate boxes
the space between them
charged
waiting till the feeling
should return.

III

but she was known to be
unwise
and lovesick lover of motionless
things
wood and bits of clever
stone
a tree she cared for swayed overhead
in swoon
but would not follow
her.

IV

and his fingers peeled
the coolness off
her mind
his flower eyes crushed her
till
she bled.

# Gift

You intend no doubt
to give me nothing,
and are not aware
the gift has already been
received.
Curse me then,
and take away
the spell.
For I am rich;
no cheap and ragged
beggar
but a queen,
to rouse the king
I need in you.

# Clutter-up People

The odd stillness of your body
excites a madness
in me.
I burn to know what it is like
awake.
Arching, rolling
across
my sky.
Your quiet litheness
as you move across the room is
a drug
that pulls me
under;
your leaving slays me.
Clutter-up people
casually track
the immaculate
corridor/passion
of my death
and blacken the empty air
with talk of war,
and other too comprehensible
things.

# Thief

I wish to own only the warmth
of your skin
the sound your thoughts make
reverberating off the coldness
of my loss
to love you purely
as I love trees and
the quiet sheens and
colors
of my house
my heart is full
of charity
of fair play
although on other
occasions
it has been acknowledged
I am a thief.

## Will

It does not impress me that I have
a mind.
Chance amuses me.
Coincidence makes me laugh
out loud.
Fate weighs me down
too heavy.

When I can't bear not seeing
you another second,
I send out my
*will;*
when it brings us face to
face,
*there*'s an invisible power
I respect!

# Rage

In me there is a rage to defy
the order of the stars
despite their pretty patterns.
To see if Gods who hold forth now
on human thrones
can will away my lust
to dare
and press to order the anarchy
I would serve.

The silence between your words
rams into me
like a sword.

## Storm

Throughout the storm and party
you chose to act the child
a two-year-old as distant as
the moon.
But our thunder and lightning God
obscured the age,
revealed the play,
and distinctly your age-old glance
shook the room.

# What the Finger Writes

Your name scrawled on a bit of paper moves me.
And I should beware.
Take my dreaming self beyond the reach
of your cheery letters,
written laboriously with
stubby pencils and grubby
nails.

: What the finger writes the soul can read :

All life was spirit once
a disembodied groping across
the void;
toward the unknown otherness
the flesh is weak and slow
with luck I shall not live there
anymore.

## Forbidden Things

They say you are not for me,
and I try, in my resolved but
barely turning brain,
to know "they" do not matter,
these relics of past disasters
in march against the rebellion
of our time.

They will fail;
as all the others have:
for our fate *will not* be this:
to smile and salute the pain,
to limp behind their steel boot
of happiness,
grieving for forbidden things.

# No Fixed Place

Go where you will.
Take the long lashes
that guard your eyes
and sweep a path
across this earth;
but see if it is not true
that voluptuous blood,
though held to the tinkling
quiet of a choked back
stream,
will yet rush out
to aid shy love,
and flood out the brain
to make a clean
and sacred place
for itself;
though there is no fixed place
on earth for man
or woman.
It will not help
that you believe
in miracles.

# New Face

I have learned not to worry about love;
but to honor its coming
with all my heart.
To examine the dark mysteries
of the blood
with headless heed and
swirl,
to know the rush of feelings
swift and flowing
as water.
The source appears to be
some inexhaustible
spring
within our twin and triple
selves;
the new face I turn up
to you
no one else on earth
has ever
seen.

# The Nature of This Flower Is to Bloom

*And for ourselves, the intrinsic*
*"Purpose" is to reach, and to remember,*
*and to declare our commitment to all*
*the living, without deceit, and without*
*fear, and without reservation. We do*
*what we can. And by doing it, we keep*
*ourselves trusting, which is to say,*
*vulnerable, and more than that,*
*what can anyone ask?*

   —June Jordan, in a personal letter, 1970

# While Love Is Unfashionable

*for Mel*

While love is unfashionable
let us live
unfashionably.
Seeing the world
a complex ball
in small hands;
love our blackest garment.
Let us be poor
in all but truth, and courage
handed down
by the old
spirits.
Let us be intimate with
ancestral ghosts
and music
of the undead.

While love is dangerous
let us walk bareheaded
beside the Great River.
Let us gather blossoms
under fire.

# Beyond What

We reach for destinies beyond
what we have come to know
and in the romantic hush
of promises
perceive each
the other's life
as known mystery.
Shared. But inviolate.
No melting. No squeezing
into One.
We swing our eyes around
as well as side to side
to see the world.

To choose, renounce,
this, or that—
call it a council between equals
call it love.

69

# The Nature of This Flower Is to Bloom

Rebellious. Living.
Against the Elemental Crush.
A Song of Color
Blooming
For Deserving Eyes.
Blooming Gloriously
For its Self.

*Revolutionary Petunia.*

Books by Alice Walker available from
Harcourt Brace & Company
in Harvest paperback editions

*Good Night, Willie Lee, I'll See You in the Morning*

*Her Blue Body Everything We Know:
Earthling Poems 1965–1990 Complete*

*Horses Make a Landscape Look More Beautiful*

*In Love & Trouble: Stories of Black Women*

*In Search of Our Mothers' Gardens: Womanist Prose*

*Living by the Word*

*Once: Poems*

*Revolutionary Petunias & Other Poems*

*You Can't Keep a Good Woman Down: Stories*